The Joy of Living

Norman Vincent Peale

The Joy of Living

Inspiring and Practical Writings, Including

How to Meditate

Expect a Miracle

How to Live Abundantly

Be Yourself

The Courage to Face Life

Three Steps to Enthusiasm

And Many Others

Hallmark Editions

Selected by Aileene Herrbach Neighbors.

Illustrations © 1977, Hallmark Cards, Inc.
Kansas City, Missouri.
Printed in the United States of America.
Library of Congress Catalog Card Number: 76-22246.
Standard Book Number: 87529-515-0.

NORMAN VINCENT PEALE brings inspiration to millions through his remarkable ministry. He is pastor of Marble Collegiate Church in New York City, editor of the monthly magazine *Guideposts,* and author of numerous best sellers. He writes a syndicated newspaper column and travels widely for public speaking engagements. Dr. Peale's writings offer a practical guide to joyful living by developing positive attitudes through faith in God.

Live on the Happy Side

Once I found myself in a group where one individual was the central figure. He had a captivating personality, and was obviously beloved by everybody.

Later we were sitting apart from the others, talking. Always being interested in what makes humans act as they do, I commented upon his rare spirit.

"I have a good time wherever I go," he said.

"It is a gift for which you ought to be very thankful."

His reply was, "It isn't a gift, being happy. It takes hard work. For many years I was a sour, difficult individual. I saw the dark side of everything until a friend gave me a scolding. After thinking it over, and doing a lot of praying, I determined to cultivate the happy side of life."

I've always been thankful for that conversation, because it taught me that to *live* with happiness we must cultivate the happy side of life.

I have known a good many people who seemingly have had everything to make them happy. But they were unhappy. And I have known people who have had very little of this world's good and yet are happy. The difference is that one person cultivated the happy attitude and another, the gloomy. It is not so much what happens to us but how we react to it that makes the difference.

There is no such thing as a Pollyanna situation. Always, I suppose, if you have a few perfect days, you can count on some kind of trouble. But whether or not you live with a happy attitude depends on your own cast of mind and the power of your faith. What you think determines what you are.

Cultivate the happy side of life. That is what the Bible tells us: *Rejoice*, it says, *and again I say, rejoice* (Philippians

4:4). Don't go around with a gloomy, melancholy attitude. Don't take a negative attitude toward life. Don't think depressing thoughts. Rejoice. Now when you really do it, you will find that the percentage of good days will greatly increase.

The late Dr. William Stidger once told about a young friend of his who was awakened by his wife early one morning. They had planned a picnic, but about five o'clock it started raining. "It is raining hard, George," his wife finally said, "you'd better go downstairs and pull in the porch furniture."

He went down and got himself half soaked. When he turned around to go back in he saw his little five-year-old boy, clad in pajamas, sitting on the door step smelling the rain. The little boy said, "Daddy, that rain smells good. I like the smell of rain." The little fellow paused a moment, then added: "Daddy, isn't this a gorgeous bad day?"

Expect a Miracle

There is a great principle of life which I have seen work over and over again. It is this: What you expect out of life you usually get.

Those who expect the worst are aptly described in Job: *The thing which I greatly feared is come upon me* (Job 3:25).

Jesus put it the other way: *All things are possible to him that believeth....ask and it shall be given you, seek and ye shall find, knock and it shall be opened unto you* (Mark 9:23 and Matthew 7:7).

A major league baseball manager told me once that he learned the hard way how to deal with his players. Once during a close game, he went out on the field to tell his pitcher what to throw to the opposing batter. "Don't give him anything high to hit," the manager warned. The pitcher, obviously obsessed by the negative suggestion, threw a high ball and the batter hit a game-winning home run.

From then on, in a similar situation, the manager would say, "Pitch him low and you'll get him out." This worked much better. In fact, the manager learned that when he let a player know he expected him to play well, he usually did.

The word "expect" is defined in the dictionary as to consider probable or certain. This expectancy of good, joined with a prayer asking for God's help, will give you an unbeatable combination in rearing children, running a business or redeeming human lives.

How to Change Yourself

Not many people are 100% satisfied with themselves. If anyone is, that fact in itself is a sure sign that he shouldn't be. Most of us, when we tell ourselves the unvarnished truth, know very well there are things about us that need changing. But we are not always certain just what should be changed, nor would we know exactly how to go about it if we did.

It follows then that one of the top experiences of life is to get a good, penetrating look into yourself. Following that, a second vital experience is to learn how to correct that which you see is wrong.

Take for example the man who told me with a wry smile, "My wife sure gave me a going over; it was pretty tough to take, but now I know it's the best thing that ever happened to me."

It seems that this man was a tense, hard-driving businessman who spread tension to everyone around him, including his family. But the chief recipient was his wife, a patient, long-suffering woman; she tried to accommodate herself to his variable moods, and to rise above his exasperated irritations. He was an unmitigated perfectionist in the office and at home. Everything had to be done just right and without delay, and if duties were put in abeyance or not done well, he would "hit the ceiling with a bang."

He admitted that he would fly into frequent and violent tirades, cursing and yelling, slamming doors, and throwing anything that wasn't nailed down. Then he would slump into depression and be glum for days. His wife endured this quietly, but it was apparent even to him that years of such emotionalism were taking toll of her vitality and her naturally enthusiastic spirit.

Then the worm turned—and with a vengeance. The wife suddenly became the personification of unleashed fury. With blazing eyes, and a violence in her make-up he never would have believed possible, she excoriated him. She told him plainly with deep and incisive honesty just what she thought about him; she painted a sharply etched picture that burned into his mind like fire.

"Then," he said with awe in his voice, "a strange thing happened. As my wife stormed on, though I saw it was agony she was suffering, suddenly I seemed to see myself; I believe I saw into my own soul. I appeared to be looking into a slowly flowing stream, and in it a hard, dark, ugly object was floating.

"I knew it was the stream of my own personality I was looking at, and in that personality was this ugly thing. This, I realized, was the cause of my trouble. It dawned on me that this dark, hard, rough, ball-like substance was compounded of my irritation, my selfishness, my hatred. I knew it for what it actually was, a big accumulation of sin floating in my deep unconscious. By the grace of God through the agency of my wife I actually, literally, saw into my own subconscious. It was a startling revelation of my deepest self. I didn't like what I saw, but it explained to me why I was what I was."

Then, continuing one of the most remarkable stories of personal change ever encountered in my experience, my visitor said, "At once I felt a sense of control that was so novel to me I scarcely knew what to do with it; I felt very gentle and understanding toward my wife.

"But the important thing is that I knew I must do something quickly about that hard thing within my soul. Unless I did, the opening in my vision would close over, and it would still be there sending off its evil influence."

I asked him what he did, and he told me in simple, moving words. "I turned intensely to Jesus Christ and admitted my own lack of power to do anything about myself. I begged Him to break up and dissolve that hard thing floating in my personality. Nothing dramatic happened but I began gradually (and yet not so gradually, for at times it seemed to happen rapidly) to feel something going on within me. It was like an infection that was healing. I believe I'm changing," he concluded humbly.

But the climax to this amazing story came later when his wife said, "My husband is so very different!" And she said this with a look of wonder in her eyes.

Are You Worried About Money?

Among the many letters which I receive I can always be sure that there will be a good percentage of them from people asking how to overcome money problems. Answering these has always been difficult for me and I used to be tempted to reply by saying that I was a minister, concerned with spiritual matters, that financial difficulties lay outside my province. But then I realized that though I could give very little advice about solving the actual money problems, I could suggest a spiritual approach.

Not long ago, a letter came to me from a young housewife who said that she and her husband were talking about ending their two-year marriage. "All we seem to do anymore is fight," she lamented.

Reading on I came to the heart of the matter. They had got themselves so tangled in installment buying that their young romance had turned from bliss into one endless spindle of bills. It became apparent to me that these people didn't need a divorce court, but rather a little straight thinking on the subject of finances.

Here are some suggestions I gave them which might be helpful to anyone looking for a new approach in this area:

1. Remind yourself that you will never solve a money problem by remaining in a state of worry. You need to think creatively and it is impossible to develop creative thoughts out of a mind that is agitated. Therefore, ask God to give you a peaceful mind through which He can send an answer to your problem.

2. Remind yourself that God will supply all your needs out of His vast abundance. If only a little trickle has been coming through to you from God's storehouse of prosperity, it may be that negative thoughts are preventing the supply ducts from being fully opened.

3. Ask yourself if you are thinking lack. There is a curious law that if you think lack you tend to create a condition of lack. Shift your thought pattern to one of abundance and believe that God is now in the process of giving you the abundance you need. Repel all lack thoughts, practice abundance thoughts. In ways that will amaze you, your needs will begin to be satisfied.

4. Seek to have complete family co-operation on expenses. Make yours a family budget to be family-spent. That is, Mary had a pair of shoes last month, so John gets a new shirt this month. Plan and pray over your expenditures as a family, and each member will feel pride and co-operation as the budget is controlled and spent on the basis of a new efficiency.

5. The word "thrift" may seem old-fashioned to some people, but I believe it is the most logical answer to most of our money problems. This, of course, may not be easy, but it is good for us to deny ourselves. Pray and ask God, "Do I really need this?" The pleasure of giving up something now and saving for the future adds delight to life. Prayer control of spending brings both financial and spiritual blessings.

6. Try this specific action. Lay out all your bills before you on the table. Then ask God what to do about them. Ask

Him for a definite plan of financing. Then make a plan of payment, economy, saving and spending on the basis of the insight you receive through your prayers.

7. Are you giving a tithe—one-tenth—to God's work? That may seem a good deal, but a tithe sets in motion forces which will bring God's abundance toward you. Meditate upon God's promise: *Bring ye all the tithes into the storehouse...and prove me now herewith, saith the Lord of hosts, if I will not open you the windows of heaven, and pour you out a blessing, that there shall not be room enough to receive it* (Malachi 3:10).

My Grandmother's Cookie Jar

American people have always been a courageous, adventurous folk, a tough-minded people who wrestled with the wilderness and struggled against all manner of adversity. Now you hear constant talk of security, of guaranteed income, of protections against all manner of potential hazards, economic, physical, mental and so forth.

I think it is wonderful that our standard of living has improved so greatly. Certainly our best economic and political minds should do everything possible to prevent depressions. But this generation also must learn and relearn what other generations have known, that there is absolutely no guarantee of security in any material thing. An old hymn says: *Change and decay in all around I see:*
Oh Thou who changest not, abide with me.

If we can rebuild spiritual security into our minds and hearts, we can meet the circumstances of these troubled times.

My grandmother was an old-fashioned woman who had an old-fashioned house in a little town among the hills of southern Ohio. She was a great soul, my grandmother, and her house was the most interesting place I have ever visited.

A few years ago I returned to her house in the little town of Lynchburg. It is occupied now by a fine woman I did not know but who soon became a good friend.

She had one of those front doorbells which you twirl and her parlor was used only on special occasions such as a wedding, a funeral, a visit from the minister or something equally painful.

On the wall were mottos: "God Bless Our Home," "What Is Home Without a Mother," and other inspirational legends. I also remembered the old-fashioned stove in the sitting room. In the winter one side of you was baked, the other side froze, especially in the mornings when you scurried, shivering, down from an attic bedroom carrying your clothes to put on by the stove.

There were other things about my grandmother's house that fascinate me to this day. For instance, the old cookie jar was on a shelf in the cupboard just at the right height for a small boy to get his hand into, which he did several times each day. I shall remember those cookies as long as I live. I never tasted any as good.

In the dining room was an old-fashioned picture. It was a print of a terribly stormy sea with the sky overcast. The scene was one of desolation except for the fact that in the middle of the picture, rising on a rock right out of the vast deep, was a great sturdy cross. Lightning flashed around its top, and at the bottom of the cross, with her long white gown floating out over the water and her tresses likewise, was a woman with a beautiful, radiant countenance. She had her arms around the cross, clinging to it. Underneath the picture were these words: "Simply to Thy Cross I Cling."

My grandmother used to say to me, "Everything else may be swept away, but as long as you hold on to the cross, you will have security in this life."

This is the point some people are missing today. Our society rests on a foundation of spiritual security. If this society starts to totter, then it will be because of cracks in the base.

Let us never forget our heritage.

Vitality

A Seven-Day Spiritual Renewal

At the start of any normal day come the drains on your vitality. There may be bad news from the newspaper, radio, TV, telephone or a letter. Worry and tension will siphon off energy. Fatigue can take over by early afternoon.

Yet if you have reasonably good health, you can move through the day with vitality and maintain it all week. But you need a willingness to change your thinking and try new things. Here are my suggestions for a seven-day experiment.

MONDAY

Begin with the *anticipation* of a good week. Key on the Scriptural promise: *For as he thinketh in his heart, so is he* (Proverbs 23:7). Don't let your mind linger over bad news; seek out the element of hope in all you hear and read. With every person you encounter today, concentrate only on his strengths and abilities. Just as negative thoughts can create a kind of chemical poison inside one's body, so can positive ideas produce health and vitality. Make a list of ten tasks to accomplish this week. Do two of them today.

TUESDAY

Focus today on the word *enthusiasm* (*en theo* means "in God"). What story or passage in the Bible most typifies for you an enthusiastic person? For instance, Zacchaeus. Study this section (Luke 19:1-10) as a morning exercise. Talk enthusiastically to at least two people today about a cause or an idea you love. Key on the passage: *For they that wait upon the Lord shall renew their strength; they shall mount up with wings as eagles; they shall run, and not be weary; and they shall walk, and not faint* (Isaiah 40:31).

WEDNESDAY

Regular vitality can best be maintained when you go about your daily activities with a sense of *rhythm*. The whole universe God created operates in a specific pattern and with a definite rhythm. So, too, does life all about us. If we overexert ourselves, we get out of rhythm and fatigue sets in. If we are lazy and listless, life passes us by. But when we can put ourselves in the creative flow of life — and learn to pace ourselves — we achieve what is called relaxed power. As an exercise read the 23rd Psalm several times and concentrate on its rhythm. In every activity during the day, conceive of yourself as being in the flow of God's rhythm.

THURSDAY

The use of *praise* is an important step in maintaining vitality. Read over Psalm 138 several times. If beset by trouble, write down verse seven on a card: *Though I walk in the midst of trouble, Thou wilt revive me.* Refer to it often during the day. Make all your prayers ones of praise to your Creator. Find one good quality to praise in every person you meet throughout the day.

FRIDAY

He who is obsessed with self will eventually lose creative vitality. The balance needed is *reverence.* Not only reverence for God, but awe and wonder over His creations. The art of childlike wonder can rejuvenate tired minds and bodies. Today key on the passage, *Verily I say unto you, whosoever shall not receive the kingdom of God as a little child shall in no wise enter therein* (Luke 18:17). Reread the story of the creation, with reverence and awe. Visit a historical or religious shrine in your area and study it as though you were seeing it through the eyes of a child.

SATURDAY

Can you go through a whole day with *joy* in your heart? Joy and vitality are an inseparable combination. Joy is not concerned with having fun; it is an inner spiritual quality that overcomes despair, pain and defeat. You cannot turn on joy like an electric light, but you can prepare yourself to receive it. *My spirit has joy in God* (Luke 1:47, Moffatt). Read through the Psalms and list five passages which show the relationship between joy and vitality. Ask God to fill you with His spirit of joy. Then go back through your week's activities. Have you completed the ten tasks you set out for yourself? If not, try to complete them today — with a joyful heart.

SUNDAY

Vitality cannot be maintained without a day of *rest*. Begin by going to church with the sole intent of worship. Drop from your mind all worries and concerns so that you can concentrate on Him. During the remainder of the day slow yourself down. Take a nap. Read. Pray. Meditate. Do something relaxing with your family. Take a walk and seek the values in nature. Carefully look at a flower or tree; chat with a friend; pat a dog. Listen to a singing brook, the wind in the trees, the warble of a bird. From this restful day will come the refreshment you need to begin another busy week.

Love Life and
Life Will Love You Back

Artur Rubinstein, the famous pianist, was once asked the secret of his success — was it dedication, ability, discipline, hard work?

Mr. Rubinstein smiled as he remarked, "It's hard to say, but one thing I do know; if you love life, life will love you back!"

What a wonderful insight! That philosophy explains how a man in his eighties can continue to be so creative. For life is simply filled with exciting blessings for everybody. They're ours if we give enough of ourselves to life!

I believe the giving starts when we get up in the morning. One man I know begins every day repeating some words from Scripture such as, *When I awake, I am still with thee* (Psalm 139:18). Then he talks more directly with his Maker, "Lord, You've watched over me through the night. Now help me do something really great with this day."

Watch what happens to members of your family when you begin the day with a glow of good feeling and joy. They'll catch it too.

The same will hold true for the people you encounter all day long, in the office, at the restaurant, in the bus, in the elevator, at the grocery store or at your neighbor's: Love life and life will love you back. Love people and they will love you back.

Make the Most of Mealtime

I remember some hectic meals my wife, Ruth, and I refereed when our three children were young. After a quiet period of grace, there was an inevitable glass of spilled milk, some dropped silverware and so on. These infractions were followed by the usual admonitions which sometimes jumped from the original offense, to dirty hands, to general appearance, to unfinished school work.

Finally one day Ruth and I decided some changes were needed. Mealtime, we agreed, should be a time to draw together, not split apart. It should be a time for quiet nourishment, fun, maybe education and possibly spiritual growth. We decided to set a different tone for our mealtimes and though we weren't 100 percent successful, we turned the tide.

Let me set down a few of the practices we followed, along with others I've learned over the years.

1. Plan the evening meal for a regular time each day. Insist that it is so important for all to be present that other activities must be scheduled around it. Allow at least one hour.

2. Begin the meal with grace, with each member taking his or her turn saying it.

3. Make this a rule: no criticism of each other. Children often dread the family dinner because this is when they get dressed down by parents or older brothers and sisters for their transgressions.

4. Parents should direct the conversation to include everyone at the table. One father I know would present a true-life dilemma at certain meals, then ask for opinions. Another device is to ask each person to describe his most interesting experience of the day.

5. Once a week have a special dish representing another country or another cultural tradition. Then use part of the dinner period for a discussion of the country, its traditions, its history. On holidays or famous dates in history assign someone to give a report.

6. End the meal with a family devotion which could include a reading from the Bible or an inspirational book. Discussion might center around how the passage applies to the family's current life and activities. The final prayer could set the tone for the remainder of the evening.

The Pace That Stills

Coming out of a reception at a New York City hotel, my wife, Ruth, and I found it was raining hard, a soaking downpour. We tried in vain to get a taxi, and considered taking a bus, but would have been drenched getting to it. Then I remembered a similar situation when I had practiced intensive positive thinking and immediately a taxi had pulled up. So I started thinking positively, hoping the same thing would happen again.

Along came an old horse-drawn hansom cab, one of those that take tourists around the Central Park area. The driver, perched on the high outside seat of this ancient conveyance, had on a great sou'wester. The rain was coursing down it in rivulets and dropping from his rubber hat.

I turned to Ruth and said, "We've been here twenty-five minutes waiting for a taxi. What do you say we take this carriage?"

"Oh, yes, let's," she said, getting in.

The driver tucked us in with a big robe. We started off. The windows of the old vehicle rattled. They were the kind of windows that stubbornly drop down when you try to pull them up shut.

Noticing the tufted upholstery, I remembered admiringly, "I haven't been in one of these things since I was a boy." But moments later I continued, "This old hack will never get us home. Think of it, all the way to 84th Street at this pace!"

However, we gradually adjusted to the pace. We plodded along slowly to the patient *clop-clop-clop* of the horse's hoofs through the rainy streets. Taxis and cars going the same way sped past us.

We proceeded north on Park Avenue. Every so often

the horse would trot for a few minutes, then walk slowly. As I sat back in the ancient vehicle, rain beating against the window, a feeling of relaxation came over me.

It was the slowest trip to 84th Street I have ever made, but by all odds, the most pleasant. You couldn't hurry, so all sense of haste was laid aside.

At last we arrived. As I paid the man, I said, "I've sure enjoyed the ride. How old is this hack?"

"It's a real antique," he answered cheerfully. "Older than I am. But," he added, "you had a leisurely, slow, unhurried drive, didn't you?"

"It was indeed all that!" I said. "I never knew one could be so relaxed in New York traffic."

We live in a tense, hard-driving generation, thinking we just have to get there in a hurry. Why, I'll never know. And it's wonderful what a little slowing down can do.

We don't need a horse-drawn carriage to slow the pace; there are other ways. The trick is to break our rhythm. One way might be to try walking to Grandma's house with the family, instead of taking the car. Or try making a real homemade cake, instead of using a "mix." We might take time to go through the family photo album slowly, reliving the pleasant moments; or take the long way to the store one day, stopping at points of interest, looking for things we never particularly noticed before.

Breaking the pattern of rush, rush, rush can restore our bodies and our minds and can bring an oasis of healing calm in the midst of stress.

Picture It!

In my counseling work with confused and unhappy people, so many times I find a sense of failure because the person wanted very much to accomplish a certain something in the world, but went about it the wrong way. "How do you go about it?" I am asked.

First, you pray about it. Why? Sometimes the things we want to accomplish aren't so good for us or anyone else. But you'll know this if you pray about it with sincerity and humility. When you pray in that spirit you receive a wisdom that by nature you do not possess.

Next, you paint on your conscious mind a picture of yourself accomplishing this thing. You hold this picture persistently in your conscious mind until it sinks into the unconscious mind. Furthermore you must visualize this achievement-process as beginning, not in some hazy future time, but *now.* And the stronger the visualization, the more immediately the process will begin.

To be sure, picturing alone won't make things happen. You have to add intelligence and planning and self-discipline and work. But it will be far easier to add these things if you have painted on your mind a clear picture of the desired outcome.

This is not just my idea. One of my authorities is William James, perhaps the greatest psychologist this country ever produced. James said, "Believe that you possess significant reserves of energy and endurance and your belief will create the fact."

I have had to learn this the hard way, because I started out in life with a king-size inferiority complex and a tendency to expect the worst, not the best. Fortunately, the Lord sent me some good teachers along the way, and one of the best has been my wife.

I remember an incident that happened over 30 years ago soon after we came to New York. We were having quite a difficult time building up attendance at the evening service in our church.

Then one Sunday night Ruth and I were driving downtown to church through the worst weather we had ever seen in New York. It was raining, snowing, hailing and blowing all at once. "There won't be anybody in church tonight. Furthermore, anyone who comes out in this weather ought to have his head examined!" I said. Ruth, quiet for some time, asked, "What is your sermon topic tonight?"

"The Power of Faith," I said.

"You are going to preach it, but not practice it," she said. "Is that right?"

"But look at the weather!" I cried.

"Well," she said, "I think you ought to look at God. All you're thinking about is how big or small the congregation is going to be. Isn't that just pride? What about the people who need the message you're bringing to them?"

"People?" I said.

"That's right," she said, "people with problems, people with sorrows, people with troubles, with fears and hates. Let's visualize a great service, filled with the power of God to lift people and change their lives."

She got me so excited that we pulled over to the side of the street and actually did just that, sat there in the car and pictured men and women being helped. We said a prayer together. Then we drove on.

When we arrived at the church, the congregation was not large. Obviously, many had stayed home because of the weather. But this no longer mattered. For the people who had come made up a great congregation, and I can still remember the feeling of electric power in the church that night.

This technique of picturing a goal can be applied to almost every venture of life.

One of professional golf's outstanding players once said, "The secret to a good shot is seeing the ball going where you want it to, before you hit it." And many a pianist will tell you that it's possible to practice a number in one's mind without being anywhere near a keyboard. You just need to see the notes with your inner eye and hear them with your inner ear.

So, remember, whatever your goal, do these things: pray to make certain yours is a worthwhile goal. Then, once that is established, fix in your mind the vision of a successful outcome. Finally, hold that image and go to work, trusting God to help you realize your dream.

The Courage to Face Life

They boarded the Florida-bound train at North Philadelphia. My attention was drawn to these two appealing young girls because of the wide-eyed, scared look on their freckled little faces. They looked very lovable and pathetic. One was about twelve, and the other ten years old. The older girl sat in the vacant seat beside me, and her sister sat across the aisle.

I studied my seat companion for a moment for I noticed that her lip trembled and tears glistened on her eyelids. She was a very sweet youngster and the solemnity of her sadness made her even more so. She stared straight ahead.

"Going to take some pictures?" I asked, referring to an inexpensive camera clutched in her hand.

No immediate reply came. Then in a low tone she said something which could barely be heard. I asked her to repeat it and she said, still very softly, "It's awfully hard to leave those you love." She hesitated, struggling with herself. "I made up my mind not to cry. I'm not crying, am I?"

"You're doing fine. And who are you leaving that you love so much...your parents?"

"Our grandparents," she replied tenderly. "I love them so. But God will take care of us." Her voice was getting sturdier.

"And where are you going?"

"To St. Petersburg to live with our father."

"And have you seen your father lately?" I asked.

"Not for three years," she replied.

"You will like St. Petersburg with its golden sun, its gleaming blue water and its soft, sandy beaches. St. Petersburg is full of kindly people, too," I told her. "Your father will be glad to see his girls. So go down there and make him happy."

She smiled sweetly. We had reached my stop at 30th Street, Philadelphia, and when I stood up to leave, she shook my hand with real dignity. "You are right about God taking care of you both," I said. "Just put your hands in His and walk along with Him always."

I watched the long, sleek train pull out, and I must admit I felt a little choked up by this little life drama. Two half-scared little girls facing a big change in their young lives, but meeting it with faith in God.

Those girls have one thing very much in their favor as they move out into life's uncertainties. They have courage. In fact, life can be quite miserable without courage. Shakespeare wrote, "Cowards die many times before their deaths. The valiant never taste of death but once." The person who is full of fear dies a thousand deaths, but the courageous person dies only once.

When I was a boy just out of college I had the privilege of working for a great human being, the late Grove Patterson, editor of the Toledo *Blade.* I was a cub reporter under him on the old Detroit *Journal* which he also edited. He once said to me, "Get courage, Norman. Whatever else you do, get courage. Never be afraid of any person or any thing. Do not be afraid of any situation. There is only one fear you should have and that is the fear of God. Have a respectful reverence for God, but don't have any other fear."

Knowing how difficult it is to have no fear of people, of things or situations, I asked how this could be done. And I recall to this day the words he spoke and the way he looked when he said them. That battered editorial office on Jefferson Avenue seemed to light up when he spoke.

"*Be strong and of good courage; be not afraid, neither be thou dismayed: for the Lord thy God is with thee whithersoever thou goest*" (Joshua 1:9). Then he added, "Let those words and the quality of faith they express sink deeply into your mind and you will draw courage from them." And indeed I have found it to be so.

An important courage-building element is stated in that Scripture, namely, that we must *act* strong. And the simple fact is that the more you think strong thoughts and make strong decisions, the stronger you will become. This will help you grow into a person who is never dismayed. As physical muscles can be strengthened through exercise, so may moral and spiritual muscles be developed by exercising the mind through right-thinking.

The ultimate element in courage-building is the fact that we are never alone. The great God, who made and controls all things, is actually with us always. It makes no difference what we have to face, He is always right there to help. This being so, how can we lose, how can we fail?

Say over to yourself every day the powerful Bible passage quoted above. Say it until it takes hold of you. It can give you the courage to face life.

The Possibilitarian

A man I have always greatly admired was the late Charles F. "Boss" Kettering, scientific genius of General Motors. The creator of the self-starter, the Duco paint process for automobiles and many other modern devices, Kettering was one of the most stimulating thinkers I ever knew.

To his aides at General Motors Kettering often said, "Problems are the price of progress. Don't bring me anything but trouble. Good news weakens me."

What a dynamic philosophy!

I knew another man, the late Harlow B. Andrews of Syracuse, New York, who had this same kind of approach. "Let's see what possibilities there are in this situation," he would say, while others sat around taking dismal views of everything.

It was amazing how often he found possibilities too, and then the gloom artists would wonder why they hadn't seen them. The answer was that the possibilitarian was always looking for answers and they never were. You usually find just about what you really look for.

Harlow Andrews, whom I like to call a possibilitarian, was a wholesale grocer, a banker and an inventor. Some say he invented the electric dishwasher. I recall his wife complaining about the number of dishes he broke while experimenting with this "contraption." He had one of the first supermarkets in the United States. Years ago, he brought perishable food from California to Syracuse by fast refrigerated train and sold it five days later in his store. They say he used to drive the fastest horses in Syracuse — not so much because he liked speed, but because he was always hurrying to keep engagements with people who needed his help. In wintertime, he would enter the sleigh races on Onondaga Lake. Though he had had but three grades of schooling, he was a dauntless man, rugged, wise and urbane.

You just couldn't disturb this man with difficulties no matter how high you piled them. He never seemed to have more fun than when he went into action against a tough problem.

Much of his wisdom, I know, came straight out of the Holy Bible. He knew it from cover to cover, lived with its characters and marked the most unusual and striking comments on the page margins of his Bible.

The big question isn't whether you have problems; the all important factor is your attitude toward problems. How you think of the problem is more important than the problem itself.

If you want to be a possibilitarian, visualize your difficulty realistically as a challenge to your intelligence, to your ingenuity and to your faith. Then ask God for insight and guidance in dealing with the hard fact. Keep on praying and believing. Know there is an answer and, with God's help, you will find it.

The Power
of a Beautiful Scene

There was a period some years ago when I foolishly allowed myself to become overinvolved in a series of activities. I became so tense that it was impossible to rest during the day. I had trouble sleeping at night even though greatly fatigued.

Finally, things got so hectic that my wife, Ruth, and I took a week off and went to Atlantic City to try and unwind. From the window of my hotel room that first morning I could look out directly upon the sea as it washed gently on soft shores of sand. It was very quieting to behold this scene.

The day was overcast with drifting fog and clouds. Imperturbably the sea rolled shoreward with its deep-throated roar and ceaseless but perfect rhythm. Clean spume blew from its wave crests. Over the beach and climbing high against the blue sky and then sliding down the wind with ineffable grace, sea gulls soared and dived.

Everything in this scene was graceful, beautiful and conducive to serenity. Its benign peacefulness laid a healing, quieting touch upon me. I closed my eyes and discovered that I could still visualize the scene just as I had beheld it. There it was as clear cut as when actually viewed by the eye. It occurred to me that the reason I could "see it" with my eyes closed was because my memory had absorbed it.

In the days that followed I discovered that the regular contemplation of beauty had a healing effect on the tense muscles and organs of my body. Fatigue drained away. Energy returned.

I discovered something else too. I wasn't bound by my immediate surroundings in this practice. When a storm came up, I could turn away from the ocean and re-live other peaceful, beautiful scenes from my past. As a part of this therapy I visualized God as creator of this beauty and pictured His master design in the change of seasons, in the rhythm of life.

Today whenever I feel gripped by pressure and tension, I go through this same procedure. I stop for several min-utes and remove myself from the activity at hand. Then I bring up, from out of memory's storehouse, scenes that have impressed me by their beauty, such as the time I gazed upon Mont Blanc when the vast mountain was bathed in moonlight. Or the radiant sun-kissed day when our great white ship dropped anchor off Waikiki Beach. Or that mystic evening when I first watched the purple shadows fill the Grand Canyon to overflowing with hush. Or that breathtaking morning when we awoke to find that a quiet snow during the night had draped everything outside our window in white.

This practice never fails to have its therapeutic effect. And when restless and troubled at night, seeking sleep, I review these scenes until God's quietness overcomes me and I drift into a sound and untroubled sleep.

Seeking relaxation and inner peace, of course, should never be an end in itself. The idea is not to retreat from life's responsibilities, but to build a quiet center inside one's body and soul from which you emerge each morning to enter vigorously into the day.

What are the most beautiful scenes of your past life? Create your own storehouse of memories, not only to help you find rest and relaxation, but to have more energy for daily living.

How to Meditate

Early in my ministry I was called upon to give guidance to a young couple of my church and I wanted to be sure that I would tell them the right thing. Seeking confidence, I went to Dr. Myron Simpson, professor at Syracuse University, a wise, old man who uniquely combined the philosophical and the practical.

He looked at me speculatively from behind his big oak desk as I told him what was on my mind. Then he leaned back and uttered a phrase I've never forgotten:

"Let's take a little time to meditate, ruminate and cogitate on this matter."

Watching him, I felt relaxation come over me. Somehow I knew this man would supply what I needed. He said:

"At these moments, Norman, there's just one thing to keep in mind, we can be sure that in His lifetime Jesus faced every situation that confronts the average man today. Now, let's examine His life and find the moment that fits our situation."

With that, he closed his eyes and became silent. I did as he was doing: I thought of the life of Jesus. But in five minutes I found myself getting restless. After a while Dr. Simpson opened his eyes.

"All right, let's see what we've got here," he said.

I was spellbound as, neatly and clearly, he linked the problem with Jesus Christ.

"Do you think we're ready to pray about this?" he asked.

We knelt and prayed. When I left I was confident that I was now able to act as Jesus would want. Months later, when I learned that the young couple had managed to save their marriage, I was grateful again for what Dr. Simpson had taught me.

In the passing years I have had many occasions to use Myron Simpson's method of meditation, not only with the problems of others but with myself as well. We are all obligated to seek spiritual growth if we are to fulfill the purpose for which God put us here. From practice, I have devised a simple formula. It may prove helpful for you.

1. *Have enough time.* Effective meditation must be a regulated thing. Examine your daily life and decide on a specific time for meditation; then don't let anything interfere. Early morning meditation can serve as a yardstick for your day.

2. *Get quiet.* Avoid noise and distractions. Meditation, like concentration, should be undisturbed. Sit comfortably in a quiet place where you know there will be no interference.

3. *Be aware of God's presence.* Realize that you are submitting yourself to God for His guidance and help. Recognize that thoughts which occur to you during meditation come from Him. In prayer, you talk to God; in meditation, He talks to you.

4. *Decide on an area for your meditation.* Your meditation should be organized. If you have a problem, compare it with a moment in Christ's life. This done, you will know clearly what you must do. But there will be times of meditation when you have no particular problem, but will be aware of some trait of character you want to improve or habit you wish to break. Look at yourself honestly, then plot your future action firmly.

5. *Concentrated prayer.* Your meditation finished, kneel down and thank God for these moments with Him. Declare your love and trust in Him. Tell Him the decisions you have made and how you intend to carry them out. Ask Him to remain with you all day, to strengthen you at each challenge.

   As with anyone you love, there will be moments when you and God may seem unresponsive to each other. Don't be discouraged. God knows the right moment to communicate with you, so continue to meditate regularly and these moments will prove to be the most enriching of your day.

How to Live Abundantly

It is a sad and pathetic fact that many people find life a dull, lackluster experience. People get themselves into ruts, which reminds me of a sign an old farmer put up one lovely spring beside a dirt road. "Choose your rut carefully; you will be in it for the next twenty-five miles." A great many people seem to have chosen their rut and have stayed in it for twenty-five years.

One of these ruts is *routine;* the same procedure day in and day out with little or no variation. That ought to be broken at any cost. If, for instance, you live on 69th Street and your route to the subway is through 69th Street, by an heroic effort of will, try walking through 68th Street once in a while! The difference will do something to you.

People are afraid of adventure. You cannot have an interesting life unless you take a risk. People come to me and ask my advice about taking a new job. Who am I to say? I usually reply, "Believe me, I certainly would take a new job if I found myself in a rut."

"But I don't know whether I can make a go of it!" is the objection. My reply to that is, "You will have a powerful lot of fun finding out. At least you seem to have the urge!"

The world is filled with poor, dull, uninteresting, unhappy souls. The answer, of course, is the need to make contact with the greatest Expert who ever lived an interesting life. He has rare skill, and if you listen to Him, and apply His principles, you too will find life rich and full and satisfying.

When you practice the clean simplicities of Jesus Christ, everything has lightness, brightness, exhilaration. Every common bush is "aflame with God."

People need fresh thoughts. New books, new ideas, new places, new activities and people. And forget yourself. The person who lives with himself all the time is in the dullest of company.

Jesus said to forget yourself and lose yourself in other people. Life for everyone can then be glorious, tremendous, and radiant. You do not need to suffer dullness, dissatisfaction, apathy. *I am the door: by Me if any man enter in he shall be saved* (John 10:9).

Salvage Those Fragments of Time

How often have we heard such statements: "I meant to write, but I just didn't have time" or "I wanted to drop in, but I've been so busy." Why is it that despite more time for leisure, people today are busier than ever before?

Is this busy-ness due to more activities, or to the failure of people to organize their time efficiently?

The people who achieve many things seldom give the impression of being busy. They have developed the skill of using relaxed power.

When they work, they accomplish their tasks with quiet efficiency. The secret is not that they work faster than others, but that they make better use of time. One such individual is my friend W. M. Krieger, a business executive, who told me once that he used the principle of "little pieces of time," to think creatively, to meditate and to pray. These idle periods of ten, fifteen or twenty minutes come at intervals during everyone's day — while one rides to work on bus or train or waits for a luncheon appointment.

One young man who commuted to work by train — a total of two hours — figured that he spent forty minutes reading the paper and wasted the other eighty. Yet, he had decided against taking a night course in law, because he didn't have the time.

The solution came to him: use the eighty extra minutes a day on the train to take a correspondence course in law. Riding back and forth fifty weeks the first year he constructed forty full days for this work. Of course it took a long while to complete the course, using these little pieces of time, but he would never have done it otherwise. Today he is a partner in his firm.

Many people cannot find time to write messages of appreciation to friends and family. A salesman solved this by having personal post cards printed, which he carried at all times. Whenever waiting for transportation, for a client, or during other idle moments, he would pen a few short, warm notes.

A suburban homemaker, whom we'll call Mrs. Peters, faced the fact one day that her disorganized busy-ness was about to break up her marriage. Tired of coming home to an over-weary and querulous wife, her husband had begun working later and later. Finally, she learned that there was another woman.

The stunned wife sought counsel from her minister.

"I keep a clean and neat home," she said, "and take good care of the children. Harry doesn't realize how much this takes out of a woman."

The minister shook his head. "Most women fail to realize when men concentrate all day on organization and efficiency they yearn to come home to a wife who is simply feminine, and who knows how to be leisurely.

"If a wife wants steady attention and love from her husband, she must learn how to have time for him."

Mrs. Peters returned home, took out paper and pencil and listed as best she could not only an hour-by-hour, but also minute-by-minute breakdown of her activities the past few days. After studying the results, she saw that hours were being dissipated in extra trips to the store and unnecessary steps about the house.

As a result of her findings, Mrs. Peters made two changes in daily routine. First, each morning, after getting the children off to school, she went to her room for thirty minutes of meditation. There she read a section of Scripture, then calmly made a list, in the order they were to be accomplished, of all the things she intended to do that day.

Second: An hour before her husband was due home, she retired to her room again for another half hour of quiet. In prayer, she pictured a new love and understanding between her and her husband. Following this spiritual conditioning, Mrs. Peters gave careful attention to her physical appearance.

Mrs. Peters soon discovered that with these periods of meditation and planning she was accomplishing more work in less time and with less effort. But, most important of all, the change in herself was rejuvenating the marriage.

On what activities should we spend our time — and in what proportion? Every person cannot answer this question in the same way. As a general rule, though, one should divide time between four areas: home, work, play and the church. A person who rules out any of these areas is stunting his own growth and may be endangering the happiness of his family.

Horace Mann describes our time wasting in this manner: "Lost, yesterday, somewhere between sunrise and sunset, two golden hours, each set with sixty diamond minutes. No reward is offered for they are gone forever."

If you want to make better use of time, first ask God for guidance, then make out a plan and stick to it.

The Art
of Enjoying Your Vacation

There are a lot of people who carry their own private wars with them on vacation. For them recreation becomes, in effect, *wreck-reation.*

Well, comes the question, just how do you get the most from your vacation? Primarily, I suggest you think of it as a period of *re-creation.*

I'm aware that this isn't easy. It is surprising how many individuals there are like one young man in his thirties who told me how he hated going on a vacation.

"It's just an ordeal," he said. "I don't know what gets hold of me when I leave the city. I become grouchy and irritable, and I'm constantly calling the office to see how things are there. I try to force myself to relax, but I can't seem to do it."

"You're wasting time and money if you can't literally do what the word vacation means — vacate from yourself the stress and problems of your job."

"I know it. I know it," he said.

But I could tell he didn't really understand. Some inner guilt or insecurity about leaving his job in the hands of someone else was behind the driving subconscious force that prevented him from enjoying himself.

There are others like this young man who say with pride, "I haven't had a vacation in five years — too busy." Or..."I can't afford a vacation this year."

I used to admire such people as selfless, dedicated individuals, but now I no longer do. In our society today, there are very few individuals who, with proper planning, cannot find time and funds for a vacation. The simple truth is that a vacation is an investment in health, the vibrant, dynamic health necessary to make us more effective in the home and on the job. Periodically, the human machine needs recharging, mentally and physically.

Well, then, how do we go about this process of re-creation?

First, understand that rest and relaxation are an important part of God's Plan for you. In fact, if it helps you, think of it as a commandment, for the Lord said: *Six days shalt thou labor, and do all thy work: but the seventh day is the sabbath of the Lord thy God: in it thou shalt not do any work...* (Deuteronomy 5:13-14).

God very definitely meant for us to find time to rest and enjoy ourselves.

Then, say to yourself something along this line: "This year during my vacation I shall bring joy into my own life and into the lives of those around me."

To find this joy, the psalmist suggests: *Thou hast put gladness into my heart* (Psalm 4:7). Notice that he doesn't say, "I struggled for gladness until I achieved it." The key to having a joyful vacation is to open your heart to God so that He can put gladness into your heart. Don't struggle for a happy vacation, let it come to you in a relaxed, easy way. To many determined parents, this means that you do not insist that everything go exactly according to your plan.

These things have I spoken unto you, Jesus said, *that your joy might be full* (John 15:11). Take Him with you this summer on your vacation. Relax with Him. Let His joy come to you, and through you to your family. This is the secret of having a wonderful vacation.

When a Decision Must Be Made

It is said that history turns on small hinges. A human career, too, results from an accumulating series of decisions about large and small matters over a period of years. But the catch is that you can never know when a seemingly small decision may prove to be, from the vantage of later years, the big decision of your life.

Here are some simple steps designed to help you make the right decision:

1. Find a quiet place, sit down and compose yourself. Only a quiet mind can think at maximum efficiency and you are going to need all your faculties.

2. Make a practical start by writing down on paper all the pros and cons of the decision. Very often facts on paper look much different than when merely considered in the mind.

3. Take a helpful Bible passage and use it to condition your mind spiritually so that the mind may be receptive to God's voice speaking to you. For example, try repeating, *Thou shalt guide me with Thy counsel and afterward receive me to glory* (Psalm 73:24). Or perhaps this passage from Philippians may appeal to you: *Let this mind be in you, which was also in Christ Jesus* (Philippians 2:5).

4. Ask yourself the simple question, "What would Jesus do in this decision?" What He would do would be the right thing, would it not? Right now, ask Him to take all wrong

and error out of your heart. Remember that right can never come out wrong. To get right answers, *you* have to be right.

5. Do not hurry your decision. Weigh your problem carefully. Allow it to soak in the mind, or to change the metaphor, let it simmer. If you properly condition the mind, the decision will emerge when completely done.

6. Take just a moment to thank God for giving you the right answer, for He is giving it to you, and thank Him for the great happiness which is in your heart knowing that you are so spiritually attuned that the element of error has been profoundly lessened. You are going to get the *right* answer.

7. Do you know when you have the right answer? The late J. L. Kraft, food manufacturer, said: "I pray hard and think hard and when the time is up and I must have the answer, and I have done all the praying and thinking I can do, I just say, 'Lord, please show me the next thing to do.' Then," added Mr. Kraft, "I believe that the first idea that comes into my mind is the answer. And I have been correct a large enough percentage of times to convince me that this process is sound."

8. Having received your answer, trust it wholeheartedly. Do not look back and hash it all over again. Take it with faith and thanksgiving. If you have sought God's counsel and prayed earnestly, your answer will come up as a clear, bright light burning in the mind. You can trust it to lead you through all darkness. God will see you through.

Be Yourself

One of the happiest individuals I know is a friend of mine who has the courage and wisdom to be himself. Last summer he decided to grow a beard. When I ran into him on the street a month or so afterward, I kidded him about it.

"It's a funny thing about this beard," he said. "So many people asked me how I had the courage to grow it. They are curious about my wife's reaction and if it affects my job situation. Why are people so uptight today? They're more concerned about how others see them than just being themselves."

A few weeks later he shaved it off. "It just wasn't the real me behind all that hair," he said. The point is that he had the freedom of self to grow the beard, but also the freedom to shave it off.

Our second President, John Adams, came from the heart of Puritan New England. Yet on a hot day in Washington he didn't hesitate to dump his finery on the banks of the Potomac and go for a swim. And his wife, Abigail, wasn't above hanging the family wash in the White House dining room when the weather was bad.

People who have the courage to be individuals can usually think things through on their own and make sound decisions. They don't say, "What will people think?" They say, "What's the best way to handle this?"

The amazing fact is that God created each one of us as a separate, unique person amid billions of other separate, unique individuals. So the best way to achieve real fulfillment is to be yourself.

Spiritual Opportunity in Routine Activities

I find most people today are looking for ways to apply their faith to daily living.

Here are some suggestions which, when followed, can invest even the smallest and most routine details with spiritual meaning.

When you read in the newspaper an account of sorrow, tragedy or evil in someone's life, pause and pray for that person. In this way you compassionately identify yourself with human sorrow and become a channel through which God's grace may be extended. See people, always, in terms not of what they are but what, by God's grace, they can become.

When you read of critical conditions in national or international affairs, especially those emphasizing potential negatives, counter by the affirmation of a positive attitude. Ask that God's will be done in all human affairs and offer a prayer that He may use you as an instrument of His will. In reading of great special problems we tend to say, "I am only one person. What can I do?" Well, you can pray and think and speak.

Employ spiritual strategy in your letter writing and telephone calls. Before writing a letter say a prayer, "Lord, help me to say what You want me to say." As you stamp and seal the letter and drop it in the mail box, bless it in Christ's name and bless the person to whom it is addressed. When you telephone anyone, after dialing say, "Lord, bless this conversation." When you pay a bill thank God for material blessings and bless the store owner and the clerks, too.

While driving your car, if you become annoyed by impolite and careless actions on the part of another driver, try remaining affable and send up a sincere prayer for him.

If you are a housewife, "sprinkle" some love and faith on the clothes you are washing and ironing. Put a dash of both into the meals you cook. And, as you go about your housekeeping, bless every room with the peace of God.

If you are a businessman, bring to mind each person with whom you work, and pray specifically for him or her. Try to condition your office or shop activities with prayer attitudes. Friction and annoyance are bound to arise but they won't get out of hand when there is present a basic spiritual attitude.

These are spiritual action techniques for routine events of the day. Their use will make your day a good day.

Three Steps to Enthusiasm!

Not long ago I had a glorious experience with the power of enthusiasm. I had just preached a sermon on the topic. I told the people what a wonderful life Jesus Christ could make for them. Then the congregation stood and sang "Onward Christian Soldiers," following which our organist surged into that great hymn called the Doxology, "Praise God from Whom all blessings flow."

Well, I found myself so enthused that I could hardly refrain from starting another sermon. I didn't think that would be particularly welcome with the ladies who had a roast in the oven so I restrained the impulse. I could not resist, however, having one more word. So while the congregation stood awaiting the benediction, they were surprised to hear me say:

"Friends, we have just sung two of the mightiest hymns ever written. At this moment we are lifted in mind and spirit. The immense power of enthusiasm is alive within us. Let us now go out into the world and live in that power."

Believe me, enthusiasm was working for everyone in that church at that moment. The sun poured in through the windows onto the people, but it was no match for the light that poured out from within them. It was an unforgettable moment.

Not long afterwards, at a national sales conference in Chicago, the manager of one of the companies represented asked me if there were any way I could spark one of his salesmen. "Frank needs someone to build a fire under him," he said.

"Better to build a fire in him, don't you think?" I replied.

The manager wanted to know how I proposed doing that, and I couldn't help remembering the unusual church service where we all had had fires built in us.

"Ask Frank to come up and see me," I said. "I want to try an experiment."

My object that afternoon was not to try making a great salesman out of an indifferent one; it was rather to help a man come fully alive. I knew that as he began to participate vibrantly in life, the selling would take care of itself.

There was a knock on the door—the poorest, most apathetic little knock I ever heard.

"I don't know why my boss thinks he can make a big producer out of me," Frank began. I laughed and welcomed him in.

"You *don't* have much of an opinion of yourself, do you?" I said.

"I've never been able to whip up much enthusiasm," he answered.

"But that's not the way to get enthusiasm, Frank— 'whipping' it up. Enthusiasm comes *to* you. It is the natural result of certain ways of living and thinking." And then I told Frank about that exciting church service. "You just keep that one service in mind, Frank. It contains the seed for vibrant living. Look at the three steps involved...."

First is the step of putting oneself into contact with vitality. The sermon, I pointed out, had been on the subject of enthusiasm. For half an hour we had thought on the subject, read inspiring passages from the Bible and from secular books. Then we had sung. Not a dull plodding hymn, but a march, "Onward Christian Soldiers." Just the name starts my blood racing. We had been stirred by having been in contact with enthusiasm.

Second, praise the Lord! That wonderful Doxology can put enthusiasm into anybody if he will just *do* what the hymn says: "Praise God from Whom all blessings flow!" Do it deliberately.

That afternoon I had Frank walk about my hotel room looking for things he could thank God for. It was slow-going for a while, but finally he got the picture. He began with his health, then his home and his job and his friends.

"Look at this sunshine pouring into this room," he finally exclaimed. "And that great Michigan Boulevard out there with the blue lake behind. I get the idea. It's thinking thankfully."

"That's it," I agreed. "But it's not the biggest step of the three."

Third—Put God into every thought. That's what en-thusiasm means in Greek: "to put God into." That Sunday I had talked about what a wonderful life Jesus Christ could make for us if we kept Him in the center of everything we thought, read and said. Christ's spirit is the most vitalizing energy ever created. He can transform everything we do from dull routine into a spirit-filled act of worship.

When Frank left me that afternoon I was sure he was going on to great things. I would have been able to say to him as I had to my congregation, "The immense power of enthusiasm is alive within you. Go out into the world and live that power."

The Power of Non-Resistance

I was reading the Bible before bedtime the other night and it came over me — not for the first time — that there are many statements and challenges in the Scriptures that seem highly puzzling if taken at face value.

"Resist not evil," for example. When you think about it, isn't that rather odd? Then there's that other one: "Take no thought for the morrow." Isn't that somewhat dangerous advice, an invitation to improvidence, in fact? "If a man takes your coat, give him your cloak also; if he forces you to accompany him for a mile, go along for an extra mile."

What is the Bible really saying here? What is it trying to tell us? I think the message has to do with a mysterious power that is often neglected or misunderstood by most of us — the power of non-resistance.

Only yesterday a man came to see me with a familiar complaint: nervous exhaustion. "The doctors say there's nothing wrong with me," he said, "but I'm tired — desperately tired — all the time. I just don't seem to have enough energy to do anything enthusiastically or well. I've tried curtailing my activities to the point where I'm only doing a fraction of what I used to do. But I'm still tired."

"Obviously, then," I said, "your fatigue isn't caused by the number of things you're doing. It must be the result of some maladjustment or dislocation in you. Tell me about yourself."

What he told me about was a dismal series of problems. He was worried about his children, worried about his job, worried about the political situation. "But believe me," he said fiercely, "I don't just quit on these things. I keep fighting!"

Somehow, those mysterious phrases from the Bible

came into my mind. "Maybe," I suggested, "you should try not fighting for a change."

"You mean," he said incredulously, "I shouldn't oppose things that I think are wrong?"

"Well," I said, "it seems to me that your resistance isn't changing any of the problems you mentioned. It's just wearing you down and making you less capable of dealing with them. So perhaps what's needed is some change in your attitude where these things are concerned."

He looked quite angry. "Are you asking me to be a weak-kneed compromiser?"

"No," I said. "I want you to keep your ideals and principles as high as possible. But at the same time I'd like you to experiment with a kind of relinquishment. Stop resisting these problems so furiously in your mind. Stop struggling to solve them yourself! I think that if you do, a great sense of peace followed by a great sense of power will come to you."

He shook his head slowly. "I don't understand that."

"I don't understand it fully either," I told him. "I'm not sure that anybody does. But on some deep level, this voluntary act of relinquishment seems to bring about amazing changes in people. When it goes deep enough, non-resistance seems to remove certain blocks and limitations in the human mind or soul. It opens an invisible window and lets vast creative and healing power come through."

"How can I learn more about this non-resistance business? Is there anything specific I can do?" he asked.

"Why, yes," I told him. "You can practice non-resistance, starting with a half hour each day. Find a quiet room with a comfortable couch or bed. Take off your shoes; loosen your tie. Lie down. Make your body relax. Then you must do three things.

"First, admit that your inner conflicts are draining your vitality. Face up to the fact that they exist and that they have their claws in you.

"Next, try to make your mind *let go* of its worries and resistances. Picture your tensions and troubles being drained out of you, like old, used oil out of a crankcase. Fill yourself with silence.

"Then, gradually, let healing thoughts invade that silence. Think about the power and goodness and generosity of God. Visualize the beauty of a sunset or the ocean in the moonlight. If you know some Bible passages that convey peace and reassurance, say them to yourself. If this is too much of an effort, let single words drift through your mind, words like *tranquility,* or *serenity,* or even *surrender.*

"If you'll do these things," I concluded, "even for half an hour a day, you'll begin to come back from the twilight world into which your sterile resistance-pattern has pushed you. I'm sure of it."

As I spoke, for the first time my visitor had leaned back in his chair. Now I saw that he was regarding me quizzically. "You," he said, "are a cunning and devious fellow. You didn't even mention the word, but what you just recommended is half an hour of daily prayer. Am I right? Don't evade! Don't resist! Answer the question! Guilty or not guilty?"

"Guilty!" I said. We both laughed. And the interview was over.

Three Spirit Lifters

A merry heart doeth good like a medicine.
PROVERBS 17:22

Joy has great therapeutic or healing value, whereas gloom and depression dry up creative life processes. Perhaps this is why Jesus so emphatically tells us to rejoice. One should learn to live the joy way. This does not mean, of course, to take a light or flippant view of the pain and realistic difficulties of contemporary life. But it does mean, certainly, to take a hopeful and optimistic attitude.

One can think happy thoughts, say happy things, and seek in every way to put joy into people's lives. The more enthusiastically you do this, the more strength you will give to others, the better you will help to make the world, and the more surely you will keep your own spirit high.

Be still, and know that I am God.
PSALM 46:10

In these words is a most effective technique of relaxation. "Be still" — that is, reduce your activity, stop your headlong rush, slow down, do not walk or talk so fast; in fact, do not walk or talk at all. Sit still, be silent, let composure creep over you. You are agitated and therefore momentarily incapable of those creative and basic thoughts which can reorganize your activity.

Having attained an attitude of stillness, the greatest of all thoughts will then come stealing into your mind. You are then ready to know that "I am God" — that is, you realize that you cannot do everything, that the world does not rest on your shoulders. The simple truth that you are to do your best and leave the rest to God comes back to your consciousness. Out of such self-treatment your spirit will be lifted.

Jesus Christ, the same yesterday, and to day, and for ever.
HEBREWS 13:8

The simple truth here stated is that Jesus Christ never changes. He is an invariable factor in a variable world. He alone, of all men, is not a prisoner of His date. He is just the same now as when He walked the shores of Galilee. He has the same kindness, the same power to heal and change men's lives. He is the same restorer of courage, the same transformer of men's souls.

Anything that He ever did for anybody throughout all history He can do for you. It all depends upon how completely you surrender yourself to Him, and how sincerely you believe.

Get Some Rhythm Into It!

The other day at the beach I saw a familiar sight: a car stuck in the sand. Two young men pushed frantically while a third gunned the engine. The back wheels spun futilely. Finally the driver looked back in exasperation. "Rock it," he yelled. "Get some rhythm into it!" Ten seconds later, what seemed like half the effort, the car rolled free.

Get some rhythm into it! Watching those youngsters drive away, I couldn't help thinking that there is a whole philosophy of life in those words. Rhythm means measured motion, balanced proportion, and it runs through the whole universe. Day follows night, season succeeds season, the tides ebb and flow, the moon waxes and wanes. Somebody once said that the rhythm of the universe is the heartbeat of God. If it is — and if we could get ourselves completely in phase with that great heartbeat — how satisfying our lives would be!

Is it possible to achieve such rhythm in our lives? I think so: God designed us to function in His rhythmic universe. First we have to accept the idea that there *is* such a rhythm, not only on the physical but also on the spiritual plane.

Then we have to figure out ways to link our lives to it. This can be done through prayer. By a quiet asking for His effortless power. Try staying linked to this power throughout the day. Begin by reading several Psalms in the morning. Continue the rhythm with grace at meals. Pause at intervals to express joy for His creations. End the day with a prayer of thankfulness.

There's also a kind of rhythm that flows through our relationship with other people. Suppose you dislike somebody or resent somebody or have vindictive feelings about them. If you do—and while you do—you are out of rhythm with the underlying spirit of Christianity, which is love. Suppose you are cheating somebody—your boss, your business partner, perhaps your wife. Again, you are out of rhythm with the nature of God, which includes perfect justice and perfect honesty and perfect kindness.

I believe that when you're tense or hurried or harassed or fretful you're outside the great rhythm of the universe that contains none of those things. What you're doing, really, is allowing self to get in the way, blocking you off from harmony with the universal mind. It's only when you make yourself relax, calm down, stop fretting that the power can begin to flow....

Many times, wrestling with a book or a sermon, I have felt frustration and tension build up inside of me until creative work becomes almost out of the question. When that happens, I try to remember to lean back, make myself relax and murmur, "Easy does it." Because when you're open to the great creative forces around you, work does seem easy.

This applies to any task, not just writing or preaching. I think a woman who finds herself resenting housework might well say to herself, "Easy does it. This is part of God's rhythm for my family. If I let that rhythm help me, I can sail through this."

I think a salesman who gets discouraged might say to himself, "Easy does it. Why don't I wait until my energy and optimism come back tomorrow? I'll tackle this customer then."

God's law of rhythm is available to all of us. It's like a great dynamo, ready to supply power to anyone who will just plug in.

My Favorite
Four-Letter Words

Four-letter obscenities are being used more and more in literature, movies and, so I'm told, even in sophisticated conversation. Some psychologists even suggest obscenities serve a useful purpose in helping people find a release from tension and frustration.

It's a temporary release at best, and more than likely will bring the user increasing self-dislike and frustration.

I'd like to suggest a better way to use four-letter words.

The idea comes from pharmacist George Scharring-hausen, who some years ago went through a period of intense stress and tension. A man of imagination who enjoys crossword puzzles, he began working on a written formula for inner strength. The result was a series of four-letter words to give him a healthy mental attitude all day long.

Here are the five key words:

1. *Look.* Look squarely at the nature of your problems. Be alert. Keep looking for the right solutions. Look around you for opportunities.

2. *Work.* Nothing will so fortify you against stress as hard, constructive work. It helps you forget yourself.

60

3. *Give.* Give yourself to people. Be genuinely interested in their problems — in the process you'll overcome reluctance and weariness.

4. *Love.* It nourishes and restores you. Love is taking a phone call at three o'clock in the morning, getting up to prepare a prescription for a sick child. It is going the second mile in caring for people.

5. *Pray.* Prayer connects you with spiritual power, builds up your inner strength. From it comes the certainty that you are being helped by Someone else — and that is a wonderful confidence-builder.

You don't have to utter obscenities to relieve tension and frustration. Instead, try this formula of four-letter words to give inner strength to match outer stress:

Look,
Work,
Give,
Love,
Pray.

*Set in Janson, a typeface
designed by Nicholas Kis about 1690.
The paper is Hallmark Ivory Vellux.
Designed by Lilian Weytjens.*